A Black Hole Is NOT a Hole

Are you sure about that?

Carolyn Cinami DeCristofano

Illustrated by **Michael Carroll**

ini **Charlesbridge**

To Alyssa Mito Pusey, who heard a book's worth of possibility in a short conversation. Working with you is one of my greatest professional joys and privileges.

I would also like to express my deep respect and appreciation to Judy O'Malley. Her experience, vision, and vitality helped shape this book.—C. C. D.

To Caroline, Andrew, and Alexandra, the stars in my life; and to my cars, the financial black holes of my universe.—M. C.

Updated edition 2021
First paperback edition 2017
Text copyright © 2012 and 2021 by Carolyn Cinami DeCristofano
Illustrations copyright © 2012 and 2021 by Michael Carroll
All rights reserved, including the right of reproduction in whole or in part in any form. Charlesbridge and colophon are registered trademarks of Charlesbridge Publishing, Inc.

At the time of publication, all URLs printed in this book were accurate and active. Charlesbridge, the author, and the illustrator are not responsible for the content or accessibility of any website.

Published by Charlesbridge
9 Galen Street
Watertown, MA 02472
(617) 926-0329
www.charlesbridge.com

Library of Congress Cataloging-in-Publication Data
Names: DeCristofano, Carolyn Cinami, author. | Carroll, Michael, illustrator. Title: A black hole is not a hole: updated and expanded edition / Carolyn Cinami DeCristofano; illustrated by Michael Carroll.
Description: Updated and expanded edition. | Watertown, MA: Charlesbridge, 2021. | Includes bibliographical references and index. | Audience: Ages 9–12 | Audience: Grades 4–6 | Summary: "An accessible introduction to black holes: what they are, how they form, and how scientists find them. This expanded edition includes updated facts and a new chapter on the first-ever photograph of a black hole."—Provided by publisher.
Identifiers: LCCN 2020055951 (print) | LCCN 2020055952 (ebook) | ISBN 9781623543082 (hardcover) | ISBN 9781623543099 (trade paperback) | ISBN 9781632899606 (epub)
Subjects: LCSH: Black holes (Astronomy)—Juvenile literature.
Classification: LCC QB843.B55 D43 2021 (print) | LCC QB843.B55 (ebook) | DDC 523.8/875—dc23
LC record available at https://lccn.loc.gov/2020055951
LC ebook record available at https://lccn.loc.gov/2020055952

Printed in China
(hc) 10 9 8 7 6 5 4 3 2 1
(pb) 10 9 8 7 6 5 4 3 2

Illustrations done in acrylics and Adobe Photoshop
Type set in Palatino, Palatino Informal Sans, and Blambot
Color separations by KHL Chroma Graphics, Singapore
Printed by 1010 Printing International Limited
    in Huizhou, Guangdong, China
Production supervision by Jennifer Most Delaney
Designed by Susan Mallory Sherman and Connie Brown

Table of Contents

Where to begin?

YIKES!

Introduction

Have you heard the news?

In outer space, mysterious entities called black holes seem up to no good.

From the headlines, you'd think black holes were beasts with endless appetites, lying in wait for the next meal. By some reports they are "runaway," out-of-control "predators" that "feed" on galaxies, only to "belch" and "spit out" what they don't eat. They "lurk" in the shadows, "mangling" stars and "gobbling" them up. In short, they have a nasty reputation for being monsters "gone mad."

But you know what?

A black hole isn't a monster. It's not even alive. That means it can't lurk, eat, or belch. It has no dark, destructive desires.

Of course, you may have already figured this out. But you know what else?

A black hole is NOT a hole—
at least not the kind you can
dig in the ground
or poke your finger through.
You can't just walk along
and fall into one.
A black hole isn't a hole
like that.

If a black hole is not a hole,
then what in the universe is it?

Places with Pull

A black hole is a place in space with a powerful pull.

Way out beyond where you are right now, beyond the clouds, beyond the Moon, beyond Pluto, beyond our solar system, space goes on and on. You could travel for trillions of miles and you'd barely get to the closest star. In another few trillion miles, you might pass another star. Space is that huge.

Way out there—trillions, quadrillions, and even more *-illions* of miles away—are special places called black holes. These places in space are special because of their powerful pull on other things. A black hole's pull is the strongest pull in the entire universe.

Nothing can out-tug a black hole. No army of tow trucks, no convoy of supersized earth haulers, no fleet of giant rocket engines. Not all of them combined.

A black hole pulls in nearby dust. It pulls in nearby asteroids. It pulls in nearby stars and even nearby starlight. And no light, stars, asteroids, or dust comes out. Not ever.

The super-pulling power of a black hole is enough to haul in entire stars. In this artist's image, a black hole reels in glowing gas from a nearby star. (The star itself is out of the picture frame.)

PLUTO

BLACK HOLE

THIS WAY TO POINT OF NO RETURN

Pluto

Neptune

Uranus

Saturn

Jupiter

How Far Out Is Way Out There?

Black holes are way out beyond where you are right now—much farther away than the edge of our solar system. To talk about the distance to a black hole, you'd need a huge number.

How huge? Well, in your everyday life, you probably travel only a few miles (or kilometers). At most, you might go tens of miles. Longer trips might be in the hundreds or even thousands of miles. In outer space, these distances would seem smaller than baby steps. Out there, you'd need to stock up on zeroes to describe how far it is from one place to another.

From Earth to the Sun: *millions* of miles or kilometers

From the Sun to the next closest star: *tens of trillions* of miles or kilometers

From Earth to the nearest black hole: *tens of quadrillions* of miles or kilometers

Distance across our galaxy (Milky Way): *hundreds of quadrillions* of miles or kilometers

Distance across the observable universe (which may be much smaller than the whole universe): *sextillions* of miles or kilometers

Hundred	100
Thousand	1,000
Million	1,000,000
Billion	1,000,000,000
Trillion	1,000,000,000,000
Quadrillion	1,000,000,000,000,000
Quintillion	1,000,000,000,000,000,000
Sextillion	1,000,000,000,000,000,000,000
Septillion	1,000,000,000,000,000,000,000,000
Octillion	1,000,000,000,000,000,000,000,000,000
Nonillion	1,000,000,000,000,000,000,000,000,000,000

In the universe, enormous distances separate even "close" neighbors. The Sun and Pluto, for instance, are a staggering 3,647,240,000 miles (5,869,660,000 kilometers) apart—yet that's just a hop, skip, and jump, astronomically speaking! (Sizes and distances in this diagram are not to scale.)

Sun

Mercury

Venus

Earth and its moon

Mars

A black hole is like a giant whirlpool.

Have you ever pulled out a sink stopper and watched water swirl down the drain? Spirals of water flow toward the center. You've made a small whirlpool.

Imagine a bigger whirlpool in a river. Far away, nobody knows it's there. Boats chug and sail along. Schools of fish dart by, following their fishy urges. Closer to the whirlpool, it's a different story.

A fish swimming near the whirlpool's edge feels a gentle tug as the current drags it toward the spinning center. No problem. With a little swish, the fish can speed up, giving itself the oomph to swim away. After putting some distance between itself and the whirlpool, the fish no longer feels the current's inward pull.

But what if the fish drifted farther in?

Closer to the center of the whirlpool, the pull would grow stronger. To escape the whirlpool, the fish would have to swim faster than it had to at the edge. Even closer to the middle, if the fish couldn't go much faster, it would find itself swept all the way in, stuck in the swirl, pulled round and round and round.

A black hole works something like that whirlpool.

Even though a black hole's pull is the strongest in the universe, it's not strong from far away. Galaxies and stardust drifting through space don't get dragged into a distant black hole.

However, near a black hole, gases and dust and stars encounter its tug. Some things may be hurtling by so fast they won't get pulled into the black hole. Other things may not be as swift. They will be drawn in.

Closer and closer, the tugging force gets stronger and stronger. Close enough, the black hole no longer acts like a whirlpool.

What a drag!

The inward pull of a swirling whirlpool gets stronger near its center. The closer a fish (or anything else) gets to the center, the more speed it needs to get out.

Even though it's like a whirlpool, a black hole is not a whirlpool.

With a whirlpool, there's always a fast-enough fish— or a fast-enough *something*—that moves so quickly it won't be pulled all the way into the center.

Not so with a black hole! Within a certain distance the black hole's power is so strong, nothing is fast enough to zip away.

This is a black hole's special trait: its super-pulling zone. Outside the zone, there's always the chance that something will zoom past and away. But anything inside this zone stays in the black hole's place in space forever. Nothing else in the universe is so inescapable.

So a black hole is NOT a whirlpool. It just (sort of) acts like one.

There's another difference. In a whirlpool, the swirling current of water draws the fish into the center. But a black hole isn't made of water. Something else drives its pulling power.

Like a fish caught in a whirlpool, colorful, glowing gases swirl toward a black hole. The dark center marks the black hole's super-pulling zone. (Artist's representation)

The Pulling Power of a Black Hole

A black hole is an extreme gravity zone.

Gravity is the source of a black hole's super pull.

You deal with gravity every day. You count on it to bring you back to the ground when you jump up. You depend on it when you try to catch a pop fly, knowing the ball will fall down. You expect it to be there, even if you don't think about it much.

People must have always noticed that objects fall, but they didn't know what made this happen. They certainly didn't guess that falling objects had anything to do with the stars, Moon, planets, and Sun—but then one man came along with some new ideas.

Gravity Rules

Just outside a black hole's extreme gravity zone, its gravitation is still remarkable. In this artist's picture, a black hole pulls clouds of gas off a nearby star.

That man was Isaac Newton. In 1687 he proposed that objects fall to the ground because Earth pulls on them. But his idea reached beyond Earth. He suggested that *all* things pull on each other, even when they are not touching. He considered this pull a force of nature and referred to it as *gravitas*—what we now call gravity.

According to Newton, the force of gravity is a two-way tug between any two objects. It works with anything—any matter at all. The matter can be a tiny bit of a thing, as small as a speck of stardust. It can be a huge collection of material, as gigantic as a galaxy. It can be as rigid as rock or as flimsy as flame. No matter what it is, if it's made of matter, then it possesses the power to pull on anything else.

Newton also noted that in any situation, the strength of the pull depends on how much matter, or mass, is involved. When there's a lot of matter, there's a strong pull. Less matter means a weaker pull. For example, imagine a fluffy snowball and a harder-packed snowball of the same size. The fluffier ball is made of less stuff. Its pull is wimpier than the pull of the densely packed ball.

You can feel this difference when you hold the two snowballs in your hands. Each one presses down on your hand because of the gravitational attraction it shares with Earth. The hard-packed snowball has a stronger attraction to Earth because it is made of more material. It presses more forcefully than the fluffy one. It feels heavier.

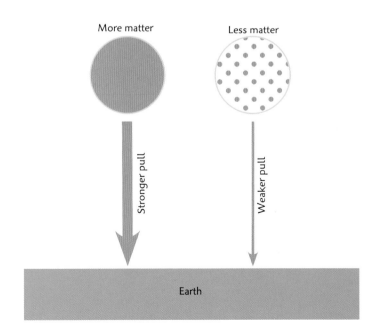

Gravity works everywhere in the universe (as far as anyone can tell). It's gravity that holds the solar system together. Even faraway Pluto and Neptune, as well as the outer comets, are gravitationally connected to the Sun. Instead of flying off into other parts of space, they stay in our solar neighborhood. The Sun's gravitational pull extends so far out because the Sun has a lot of matter packed into it—about five hundred times the mass of everything else in the solar system combined!

Even so, the Sun's gravitational reach is tiny compared to the whole universe. Most things are too far away to be swept in by the Sun's gravity. Thanks again to Newton, we know that the closer things are, the harder they pull on each other, and the farther apart they are, the weaker they pull.

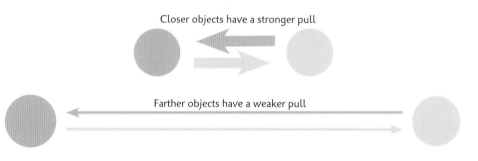

Closer objects have a stronger pull

Farther objects have a weaker pull

This is true for all matter in the universe, including black holes. It's just that with black holes, the close-up effect is extreme.

Facts of the Matter

How densely packed is the material that forms a black hole? Imagine a black hole the size of a snowball. Now compare it to a "snowball" made of different materials.

A snowball-sized	Has a mass of	This weighs about the same as
Ball of fluffy snow	37 grams	A slice of bread
Ball of hard-packed snow	87 grams	A small candy bar
Rock (granite)	287 grams	A rock, of course!
Ball of plasma from the Sun's center	29,000 grams	An 8- or 9-year-old human
Black hole[‡]	50 octillion grams	10 Earths

[‡]In a black hole the size of a snowball, most of the "snowball" would be empty space (the extreme gravity zone) surrounding a densely packed center. The center would contain all the mass, yet take up less room than a single snowflake.

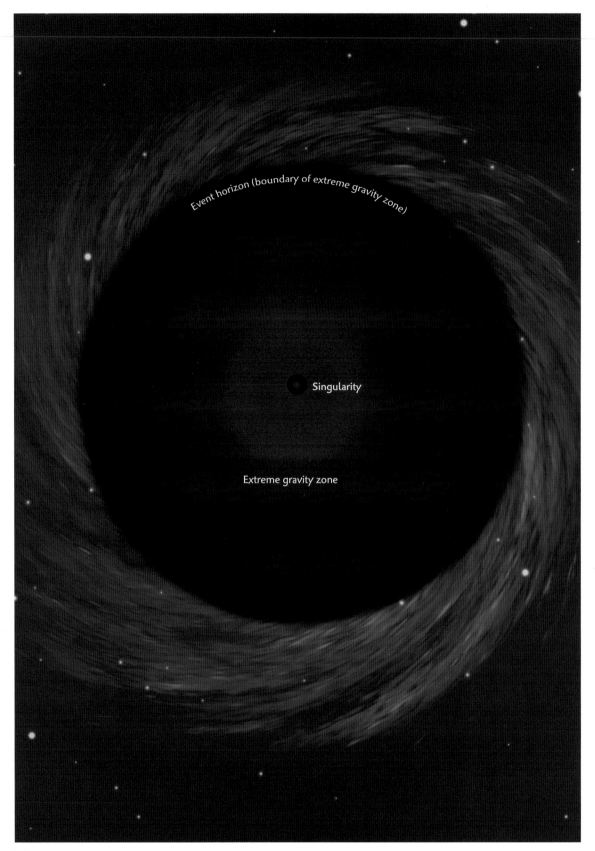

An Extreme Case of Gravity

Remember that super-pulling space around a black hole—the one with the strongest pull in the universe? That super pull is the close-up gravitational power of a black hole. Here in this zone, the gravity is so intense that nothing can move fast enough to fly, launch, jump, or zoom away.

Around this extreme zone is a boundary called the event horizon. This boundary acts like a point of no return. Once past it, there's no going back. Only black holes have such extreme gravity zones, and only black holes have event horizons. This is what makes a black hole different from everything else.

But a black hole is more than just a gravity zone—more than just empty space inside an event horizon. A black hole also includes the source of its tremendous gravitation: a massive amount of densely packed matter sitting at its center. The matter is so densely packed that it forms a single point, called a singularity.

Where does this matter come from? How did it get to be so densely packed? And what does it have to do with the beginning of a black hole?

The answers may lie in the stars.

This cross-section diagram shows the anatomy of a black hole. At the center is an extremely small, densely packed singularity, super-enlarged for visibility. Surrounding the singularity is an extreme gravity zone, colored red. The outer boundary of this zone is the event horizon. (Diagram not to scale)

An Event What?

Have you ever watched the Sun set? After it sinks below the horizon, Earth blocks your view of it. Even though you know it's still out there in space, you can't see it. Any and all events on the Sun remain invisible to you for as long as it is below the horizon. If the Sun suddenly turned purple, you wouldn't see it happen.

In a similar way, once an object enters the extreme gravity zone of a black hole, the object disappears from view. Even though nothing physically blocks our sight, once the object is beyond the boundary of the zone, we cannot see what happens to it. Events beyond the black hole's "horizon" are invisible to us. Because of this visual effect, scientists named the boundary the *event horizon*.

What happens below the horizon stays below the horizon.

3

Black-Hole Beginnings

The beginning of a black hole can be the end of something else.

Many black holes come from stars.

Every star has a beginning, when light first bursts from it. Then it shines on and on, for millions, even billions, of years. But every star comes to an end. And sometimes a star's final moments are an all-out frenzy. After the dust clears, a black hole may be all that's left.

Black hole to be?

Getting off to a bright start!

Ignition! Scientists keep their eyes on this bright, active spot in the sky, where they can witness new star formation. Eventually the brilliance of some stars may give way to the darkness of a black hole. (False-color telescope image)

Star Power

Before a star is a star, it is an enormous cloud of gas. At the start, wisps of gas and drifts of dust collect, their gravity drawing them together. As more stuff gathers, its combined gravitation grows stronger. Eventually the cloud pulls itself into a massive ball of material.

Under the force of its own weight, the gigantic ball presses inward. Deep beneath the surface, the intense pressure squeezes the material, like the powerful grip of a giant hand. The inner material packs together tightly. More matter mounts up on the outside, increasing the pressure on the inside. Soon the pressure in the center is so high, it ignites a booming nuclear reaction. Starlight bursts from the ball of gas. Now blazing, flaring, spewing, and spouting, the new star is a fiery furnace.

Sparking a Star

A star's fiery nuclear reaction is not really a fire. Instead, it is a dramatic melding, or blending, of atoms, called nuclear fusion.

Each atom has its own tiny center, or nucleus. Surrounding each nucleus is an electrical force field. Ordinarily, this force field repels other nuclei, pushing them away—but in a star, the nuclei meld. How come?

As the star material gathers, its inward pressure grows. The nuclei respond by zipping and zooming faster and faster, veering away from each other all the while. However, when the pressure gets high enough, the nuclei are going so fast that their speed overpowers their repulsion. Slamming together, they push through each other's force fields and fuse. As the nuclei meld, a smidgen of their matter vaporizes into energy. This creates a tremendous burst of furious noise, motion, and another by-product: star shine!

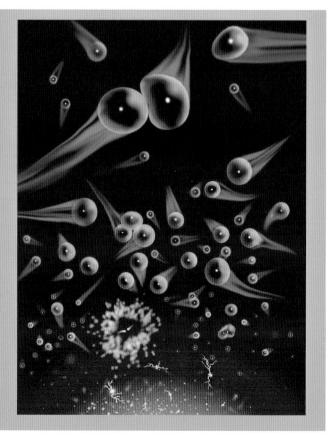

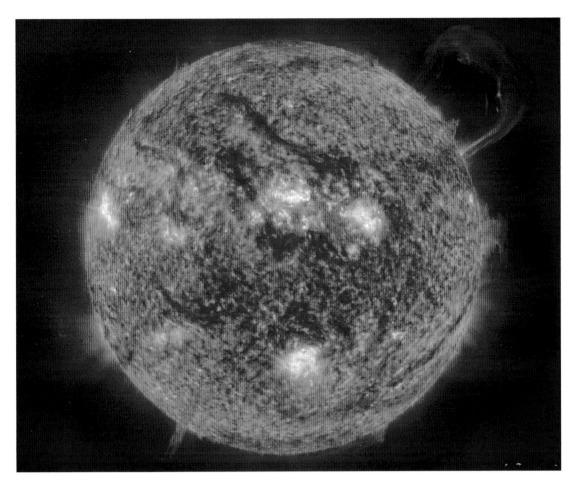

Like other stars, the Sun is a blazing ball of activity. As the brightest and hottest material rolls and swirls, darker, less-hot material sinks toward the center. The flare in the upper right is a tremendous whip of plasma lashing out into space. (False-color telescope image)

In the star's center, the gas is so energized that it has become a sort of super gas, called plasma. The hot plasma is in constant motion. It expands like hot air inside a balloon and pushes outward from the center. Meanwhile, the crushing weight of the star material continues to press inward. In goes the outer material and out goes the inner. The plasma rolls and churns like a hyper hurricane of heat, light, sound, and motion.

The star ball holds together in this perfectly balanced commotion for millions or billions of years, until the star's nuclear furnace runs out of fuel. The reaction suddenly ceases.

When that happens—look out! The end of the star is near.

Out of Fuel, Out of Time

This is a blast!

Some stars go out in a blaze of glory.

Once the nuclear reactions stop, the star's center begins to cool. The plasma slows down, its outward push growing weak. The balance is broken. The plasma collapses in on itself.

In one giant, sudden *WHOOOOOSH!*, the center of the star compresses. It caves in, growing denser and tighter than ever.

CRASH! This core material bumps—hard!—against itself.

BOOM! The material rebounds like an ocean wave slamming against a rock cliff. It pushes on the star's outer gases, which flow outward in giant surges of heat and light. As the star material rushes outward, the star grows and grows until it is a supernova, or super star. What happens next?

Possibly a black hole forms. Possibly not.

In this artist's illustration, a massive star comes to a spectacular end, its gases rebounding from the dense center and surging outward in bursts of light, heat, and motion.

In 1987 a distant star appeared as a pinpoint in the "before" picture before bursting out as the brilliant supernova in the "after" shot.

It usually depends on the original mass of the star. If the star was about twenty-five to forty times the size of our Sun, then what's left of the star's center goes into a sudden collapse, called fallback. Once again, the star stuff plunges inward under its own weight. In, in, in it pulls. Tighter and tighter the material contracts, crunching in so fast and so hard that it is destroyed. Even its atoms are utterly demolished.

All the matter that once filled the center of the star shrinks down to a single, tiny point of extremely dense mass. It has no recognizable parts. But it does have one feature that makes it unique.

It has a pull of gravity so strong that it can out-pull anything else in the universe. Nothing can out-tug it. No army of tow trucks, no convoy of supersized earth haulers, no fleet of giant rocket engines. Not all of them combined.

Do you recognize this pull? It's the pull of a black hole. The star, a big, brilliant ball of light, has turned into a dark place of enormous gravitation. A black hole has formed.

What Happens to the Other Stars?

All stars run out of fuel, but not all stars end up as black holes. Which stars form what? Here's what typically happens.

If the star is up to nine times the mass of the Sun:

Such a low-mass star never becomes a supernova. Instead, its inner core turns into a small, whitish ball of cooling material called a white dwarf. Every day you see a lightweight star that is destined to become a white dwarf: the Sun!

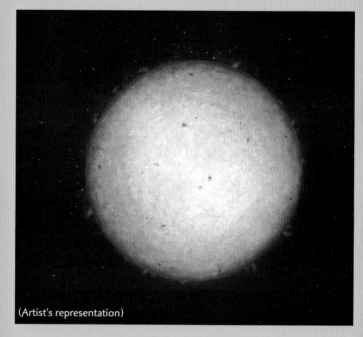

(Artist's representation)

If the star is nine to twenty-five times the mass of the Sun:

The star is not quite heavy enough to form a black hole. It goes through a supernova, but when it falls back on itself, its gravity isn't strong enough to crunch the material into a singularity. Instead, it forms another type of star, called a neutron star. Like other stars, neutron stars are ball-shaped and emit light, but they are much denser. Only black holes have a greater density.

(Artist's representation)

If the star is twenty-five to forty times the mass of the Sun:

The gases blast out as the star goes supernova. Then the remaining material collapses inward, forming a black hole by fallback (see page 23).

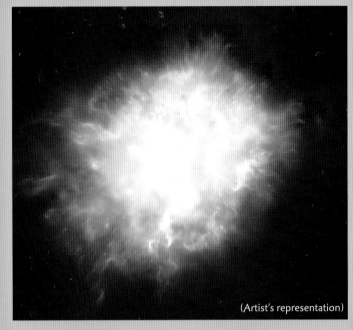

(Artist's representation)

If the star is over forty times the mass of the Sun:

When this type of ultramassive star runs out of fuel, it goes through an initial *WHOOOOOSH!* of collapse. However, because its enormous mass generates such tremendous gravitation, there's no *CRASH!* of a rebound or *BOOM!* that blasts gases out into a supernova. Instead, the matter just keeps on whooshing inward, directly forming a black hole.

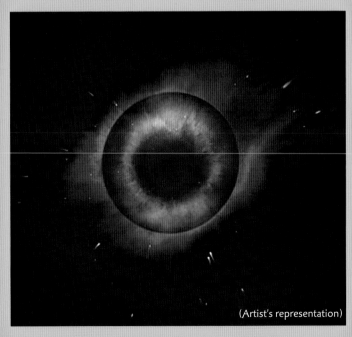

(Artist's representation)

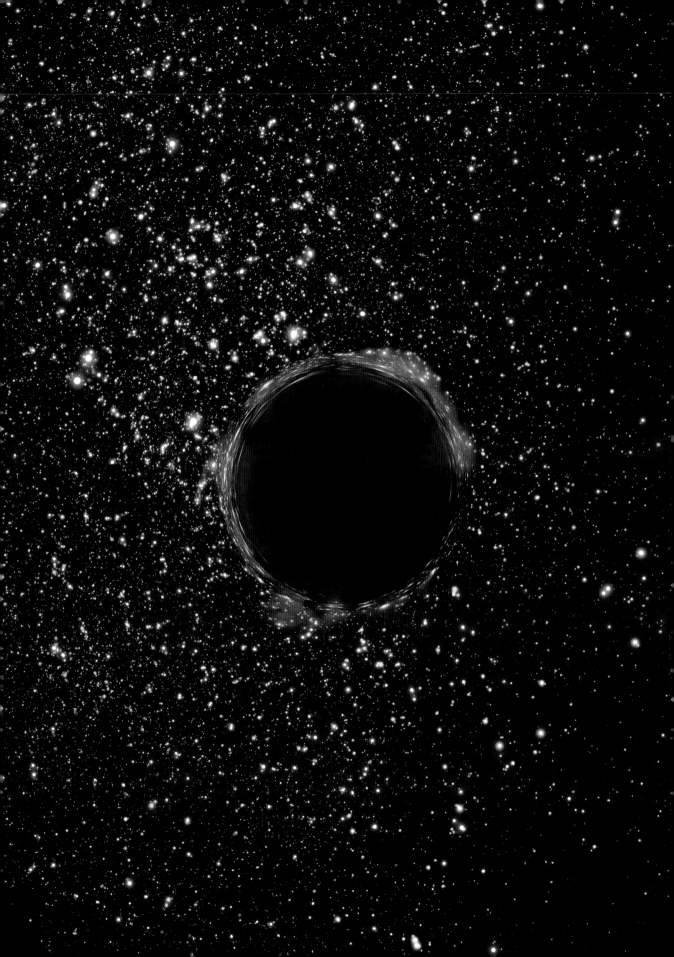

The Blackness of Black Holes

A black hole is black because no light comes from it.

A black hole is nothing to look at. Literally. If you were to paint a black hole's portrait, you'd need to stock up on black paint. *Only* black paint. Because a black hole is (you guessed it) black!

The blackness of black holes is peculiar: although there's plenty of light within a black hole, you can't see it from the outside. Yet there's no wall physically blocking the light or bouncing it back in. Instead, gravity keeps the light contained.

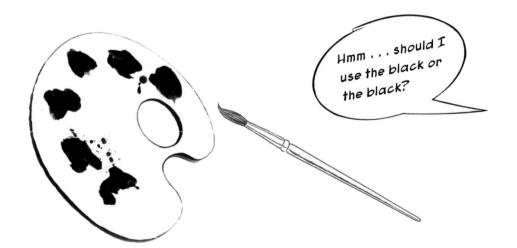

This artist's illustration helps us imagine the utter darkness of a black hole, from which no light escapes.

Moving Light: The Movie

You may not think about it much, but light moves. It travels from one place to another, and that takes time.

But not much time. When light travels, it moves fast! Our eyes and brains can't keep up. But you *can* slow down light to see what's going on—if you run what's called a thought experiment. In a thought experiment, you use your imagination to conjure up an experiment you couldn't do in real life (at least not easily). Then you run things through in your mind and see what might happen. For this thought experiment, you'll need to imagine a slow-motion movie of light. (It's okay to imagine the popcorn, too.)

It's a misty night. In the darkness, a pinpoint of light becomes visible. Someone has turned on a flashlight. The pinpoint grows to the size of the bulb. Because this is slow motion, only the bulb is bright. Nothing else lights up—yet.

Now the light begins to spread outward from the bulb. It fills a bigger and bigger space. As the light moves forward, it strikes little fog droplets, the ground, a sneaker, a tree, a cat. After each collision, some light bounces off. It is redirected. Some of it reaches a person's eyes.

Only then can the light trigger the person's eyes and brain. In slow, stretched-out speech, the person says, "Loooooo-ooooook! Aaaaaaaaaaaa caaaaaa-aaat!"

With the action slowed down, you are able to notice the time it takes for the light to move outward from the bulb to the person's eyes. This was a short trip for the light. There wasn't much going on. On longer trips, more might happen. The light might encounter places of extra-intense gravity. Then things would get more interesting. Time for a sequel! This time, the action is set in outer space.

Measuring Distances with Light

How fast can you run in a second? Six feet? A couple of meters? In that same second, light would travel more than 900 million feet (about 300 million meters). That's almost from Earth to the Moon! This length can be called a light second because it is the distance light travels in a second. (A "kid second" would be those six feet you just sprinted.)

A light second might seem like a big distance, but compared to the universe, it's puny. Astronomers need much bigger units of length to describe the stretches of space between stars. One unit they use is the light year, which is the distance that light can travel through space in a single year.

A light year is about 31 quadrillion feet, or about 6 trillion miles (over 9.5 trillion kilometers). Compare this to a "kid year"—about 26 thousand miles (or a little under 42,000 kilometers)—though so far no kid has reported sprinting nonstop for an entire year!

The Sequel: Bending Light

In *Moving Light 2,* light is on the go again, this time in a slow-motion trek through the universe. You track its path as it moves outward from a star (instead of a flashlight). Some of it bounces off asteroids, gases, and dust in its way, just as it reflected off the droplets of fog on Earth.

However, as the light passes extra-massive objects—big stars, huge planets, whole galaxies—something else happens. The light changes direction. Pulled by the objects' gravity, it veers off its straight-line course. The more intense the gravity, the more the light's path bends.

Just outside the event horizon of a black hole, light's energy keeps it zipping along, like that fish swimming along the outer edge of a whirlpool. Although the black hole's gravity changes the light's path, the light doesn't swerve into the black hole.

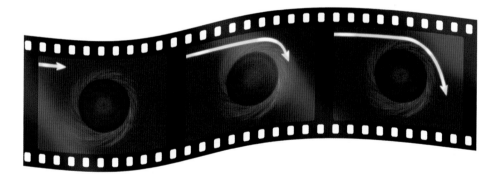

However, if light *does* cross the event horizon, the greater intensity of gravity makes the light curve inward. As the light continues traveling in its new direction, it gets even closer to the center of the black hole, where gravity is even stronger. The closer the light gets to the center, the more gravity redirects it inward.

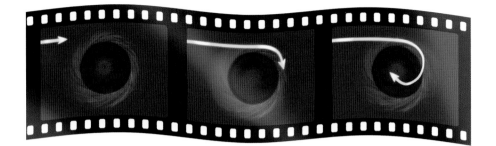

In this way, the light traces an inward spiral. Because the light never turns out again, it can't reach our eyes or a telescope. This utter absence of outward-bound light is why a black hole is black.

From the outside, a black hole is invisible. But if it's invisible, then how can we know it's there? How can we find it—especially if it's quadrillions or more miles away?

Bending Starlight? What's the Evidence?

Can gravity really change the path of light? In 1919 the scientist Arthur S. Eddington led a team to investigate this question.

The team photographed the same stars at different times: once during the night and once during the day, when the starlight passed very close by the Sun on its way to Earth.[‡] If gravity *could* affect light, the Sun's powerful gravitation would "bend" the starlight, changing its path. This change would create the illusion that during the day the stars moved slightly from their nighttime positions.

After carefully comparing the photos, the scientists announced their results: the stars seemed to have moved! This was the first evidence that gravity does, in fact, affect light.

[‡]During the day, the Sun's bright light usually washes out background starlight. To photograph the daytime stars, Eddington's team worked during a solar eclipse, when the Moon blocks the Sun's light.

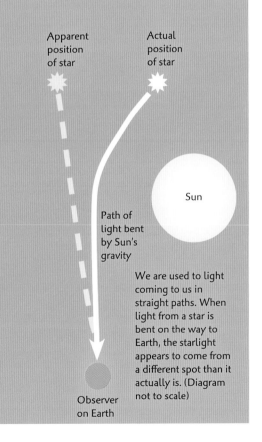

Apparent position of star

Actual position of star

Sun

Path of light bent by Sun's gravity

We are used to light coming to us in straight paths. When light from a star is bent on the way to Earth, the starlight appears to come from a different spot than it actually is. (Diagram not to scale)

Observer on Earth

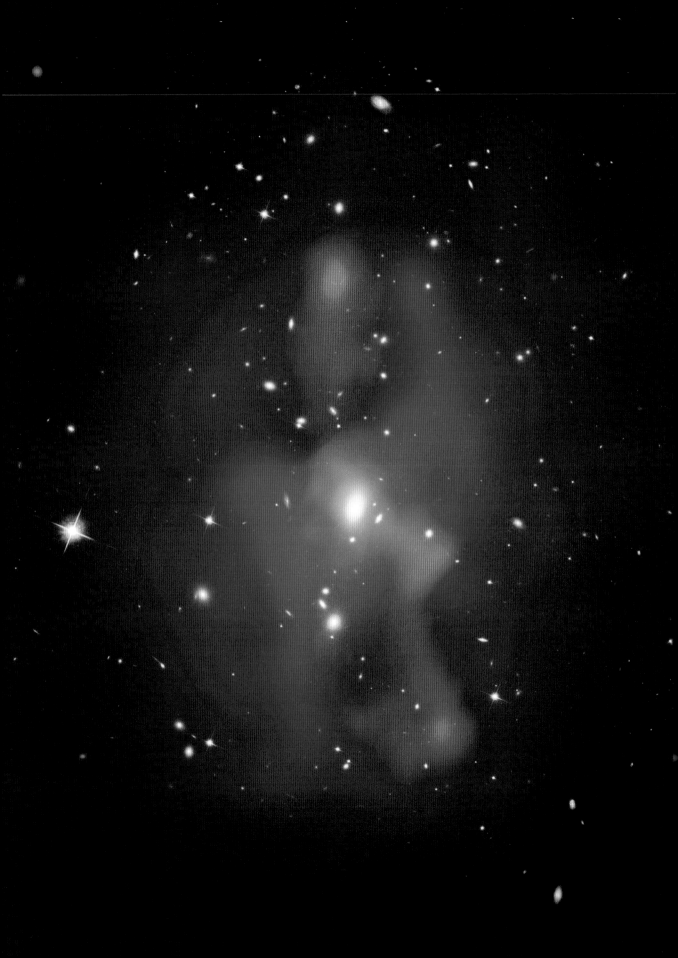

Mission Impossible?
Seeking the Invisible

A black hole is like a hiding place in space, with footprints leading to it.

There's more to invisibility than what doesn't meet the eye. All sorts of things are invisible to us, for different reasons. Some, like atoms, are too tiny to see. Others, like a black cat on a dark night, aren't lit brightly enough.

Certain things are invisible to us because our eyes just can't sense them. You don't see beams of infrared light shooting across the room from your remote control to the TV, for example, or radio waves streaming off everyone's cell phone.

Then there's the invisibility caused by a black hole. No matter how hard you look, you can't see the black hole itself. There's nothing at all coming from it—no light, no other forms of energy, and no matter. We can detect only what's around it—never anything inside.

But there *are* clues that hint at the presence of black holes. Scientists use these clues to track them, the way you can follow footprints right up to someone's hiding place.

Thanks to telescopes that translate invisible energy into color-coded pictures, we can "see" red jets of invisible radio energy fountaining from the area of a black hole.

Outta sight!

On the Trail

One of the best black-hole clues is X-ray energy. As matter approaches an event horizon, its atoms "shine" with invisible X-rays. Although our eyes can't see the X-rays, we can make detectors that respond to their tremendous energy.

X-ray-catching telescopes make pictures of otherwise invisible X-rays. The pictures reveal that certain areas in outer space are emitting intense X-rays. Each bright location points out where something extraordinary is going on. It is a hint that a black hole might be there.

Acting on the hint, scientists search the X-rays for patterns that most likely signal black holes. One pattern is an X-ray ring that seems to surround nothing. The nothing part might be a black hole. If so, the ring is energy released by super-heated matter spiraling just outside the event horizon.

X-ray rings in space can clue scientists in to a possible black hole. (Artist's representation)

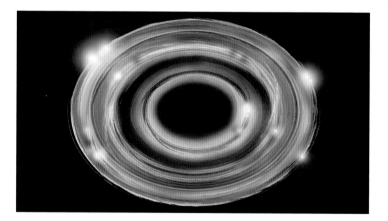

A Science Friction Story

X-rays can mark the spot of a black hole, but what generates them? Some exotic black-hole feature? Nope. The X-rays are generated by plain old friction. Friction is what makes your hands warm up when you rub them together really fast, or what makes rubber burn when a car screeches to a halt, tires skidding on the road. In the same way, material swirling in toward a black hole skids past other matter and heats up. As you might expect, near a black hole, the friction is extreme. The material heats up so much that it begins to glow—in invisible, super-powerful X-rays.

Scientists also seek patterns in the intensity of the X-rays. Just as you rely on the rise and fall of a melody's tune and volume to recognize a particular song, scientists look for a unique pattern in the rise and fall of the X-rays to identify a black hole.

Telltale signs of strong gravity may also point to a black hole. One spectacular gravity footprint appears as smudged, multiple images of galaxies. Such images can form when light from faraway galaxies passes near a black hole but does not cross the event horizon. Sometimes the galactic light splits up and bends around the black hole. Some light goes left, and some goes right. Some goes up; some goes down. The beams of split-up light make it around the black hole but may not come back together again. Like reflections in a kaleidoscope, they create multiple images of the galaxy around the black hole.

The circled blue smears in this picture are multiple images of just one distant galaxy. On its way to the telescope, the light from this galaxy passed a group of other galaxies. Their combined gravitation was strong enough to split the "blue" galaxy's light. A black hole can create the same kind of special effect, called gravitational lensing.

A star's motion can also reveal a black hole. Imagine two ice-skaters gripping hands and whirling around each other. What if one of the skaters were somehow invisible? His partner's whirling motion would give him away. Similarly, if a visible star whirls around a dark area in space, its movement suggests an invisible partner. The more intense the gravity of the invisible partner, the faster the visible star will swing around it. If the visible star cuts a fast enough orbit, then chances are good that only the strongest of gravity sources—a black hole—is there.

One telltale sign of a black hole is the incredible speed at which a visible star whips around its invisible companion. The star GRO J1655-40, shown in this artist's image, zooms around its black-hole partner every 2.6 days.

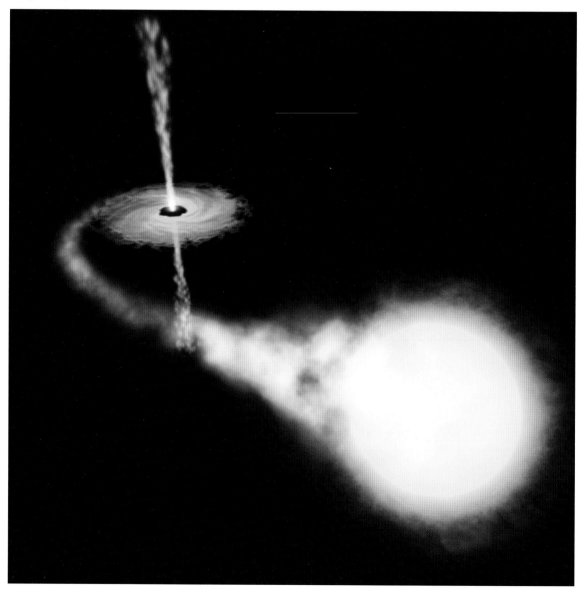

Mistaken Identities?

But there's a catch. Black holes aren't the only things that can cause X-ray rings, multiple galaxy images, and whirling stars. When astronomers discover one of these clues, they have to be careful not to jump to conclusions.

And there's another challenge. Out in the universe, finding and interpreting X-ray signals, motion patterns, and other evidence can be tricky. Reality complicates the search. It's hard to get a detailed image, even with our best telescopes. Also, between a black hole and us is a lot of space, with galaxies, stardust, gases, and more. The clues are like footprints in a crowded forest—maybe you see them and can follow them, but maybe paw prints, branches, leaves, and shadows muddle the picture.

It takes a while for astronomers to sort through these complications. Once they spy a black-hole candidate, they get to work on the evidence. How does the candidate compare to what they expect from a black hole? Are there other ways to explain what they see? If the evidence lines up just so, astronomers move from being "pretty sure" to "almost positive" they've found a black hole.

That's how science can work. But sometimes, there are twists.

Quack!

You know the old scientific saying: If it looks like a duck, and quacks like a duck, then we can safely state it is likely to have its identity as a duck confirmed at some point in the future, pending additional evidence.

6

Supersized Surprises

A black hole is sometimes where you least expect it.

One unexpected twist came as a black-hole discovery that scientists never dreamed of. The story begins with a mystery from nearly a hundred years ago. For decades it seemed to have nothing to do with black holes. The story ends with a big—a really big!—surprise.

Radio Mysteries

In the 1930s a telephone-company engineer named Karl Jansky was trying to track down the cause of hissing static in phone lines when he discovered something strange. Radio energy from outer space was interfering with the phone signals. After learning about Janksy's discovery, a radio engineer named Grote Reber decided to investigate.

What's the buzz?

Star patterns light up the night and remind us of ancient myths. In the 1900s scientists discovered that some of these constellations held tantalizing clues to a bigger story. (Artist's representation)

Reber had just one little problem. To explore the radio energy, he needed a radio telescope—a telescope that could detect invisible radio energy—but there was no such thing at the time. So he invented one. He built it in his backyard in Wheaton, Illinois. Late into the night, Reber probed the sky with his new telescope, using it to locate the source of the mysterious radio energy.

Reber mapped these signals from the sky and shared his findings. Astronomers followed up with new investigations and soon began reporting more signals. Over time, with better radio telescopes, they found that some radio sources appeared as paired patches, one on either side of a tiny dot. They called these sources "radio galaxies." They also discovered other, more starlike sources—intense dots of radio energy without patches. How strange. What could these quasars (short for "quasi-stellar radio sources") be? Were they related to the radio galaxies?

In 1937 Grote Reber built this radio telescope from wood and sheet metal. His backyard wonder launched the study of invisible light energy from space.

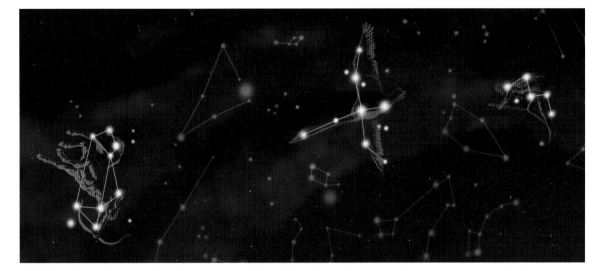

Reber found that some of the strongest radio signals from space came from the directions of familiar constellations, such as Sagittarius (the Archer), Cygnus (the Swan), and Cassiopeia (the seated Queen). (Artist's representation)

Finally, in the early 1980s, improved images revealed a stunning new picture. The radio galaxies' patches were actually the ends of colossal streamers of energy, each one stretching hundreds of thousands of light years from the center. Something powerful had to be driving these gushing fountains of energy. And the quasars? They turned out to be far, far away, yet somehow creating radio impulses strong enough to reach Earth. No star could do this.

In fact, every quasar and radio-galaxy dot turned out to be energy from the center of an entire galaxy. Astronomers found stars careening around these centers, zooming at previously unheard-of speeds in their orbits. The motion was like an accelerating ice-skater pulled around her partner in a tight twirl—or like a fish caught in a superstrong whirlpool. Something extreme had to be in the middle of each of those galaxies.

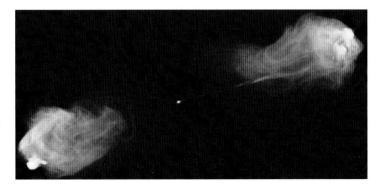

In this false-color telescope image, lobes of radio energy shoot away from the center of the radio galaxy Cygnus A. Each enormous lobe is about 300,000 light years long.

As this artist's illustration shows, matter colliding near a supermassive black hole can kick up a ruckus of energy. Such energy "footprints" help scientists in their search for black holes.

You might be able to guess what this was, but for scientists, the best answer came as a shock. In 1994 telescopic evidence confirmed the amazing cause: a *supermassive* black hole, with the mass not of one imploded star, not of two, but of millions—maybe even billions.

Imagine the excitement! Scientists had discovered a new, entirely unexpected class of black holes when they weren't even looking for one. It was like playing hide-and-seek and tripping over a whole group of people you never knew were in the game.

As it turns out, a supermassive black hole is probably at the heart of nearly every large galaxy, including our own.

Field Guide to Black Holes

Discoveries of black holes have exploded since the late 1900s. The list of finds reads like a cast of characters for a mixed-up fairy tale. At first, astronomers found small ("Baby Bear") and giant ("Papa Bear") black holes. But where were the medium "Mama Bear" black holes? It just didn't make sense that there would be smalls and larges but no mediums. Ultimately, astronomers found some "Mamas" (they think). The tiniest of all, the "Tom Thumbs" of the black-hole world, remain undiscovered, and may not even exist.

Who's been eating my porridge?

Size	What the pros call it	Is about the mass of	Forms when
Extra-extra-extra small—about the size of an atom, or smaller	Micro or mini black hole	Mt. Everest	There's no evidence—yet—that these tiny black holes exist. If they do, they may have formed when the universe began because of tiny imbalances of matter and energy.
Small	Stellar-mass black hole	3–10 Suns	A large enough star ends, either in a supernova or by directly collapsing when it runs out of fuel.
Medium	Intermediate-mass black hole	100–100,000 Suns	Stars merge and then collapse? (People are mulling this over.)
Large through extra-extra-extra-large	Supermassive or ultramassive black hole (depending on mass)	Millions to billions of Suns (supermassive) to tens of billions of Suns (ultramassive)	Stars, galaxies, and/or black holes collide? Huge gas clouds collapse? A smaller black hole grows as matter falls in over a long time? (Nobody's sure.)

You are here

Supermassive Start-Ups

We live in the Milky Way galaxy, far out on the edge of one of its spiral arms. Our part of the galaxy is relatively calm, but in the center is a supermassive black hole, a compaction of three million Suns' worth of matter.

This black hole is pretty mellow, as supermassive black holes go. Because its X-ray signal is relatively weak, astronomers didn't find it for a long time. They still don't know how it formed.

In fact, scientists are still puzzling over how any supermassive black hole gets started. Could a single supernova lead to one? Probably not. Even the biggest stars are much too puny to do the trick. To create a supermassive black hole, a star would have to start out millions of times the mass of the Sun. Astronomers

Our galaxy's central black hole is calm compared to others— but it still packs a wallop! Zooming in on the center of the Milky Way, we see a white hot spot that reveals the intensely energetic activity surrounding a supermassive black hole. (False-color telescope image)

Deep in the center of the galaxy NGC 6240, two unseen supermassive black holes are merging in a slow-motion collision. The "crash" began thirty million years ago and may continue for another hundred million years or more. The collision creates a bright splash of X-ray energy, captured here in false color.

think this is unlikely, so they have come up with other ideas. One idea has to do with crashing stars.

Near the center of a galaxy, stars are crammed relatively close together. As gravity swings them around each other, high-speed crashes are inevitable. Gravity can also cause entire galaxies to swerve together in intergalactic collisions.

When the huge amount of matter in colliding stars and galaxies compacts forcefully, it might form a mid-sized, or intermediate, black hole. With enough of this going on, several black holes might form and then pull together, morphing into one. Nearby stars might also spiral into these growing black holes, adding to the total mass. Over time, all this piling up might lead to a supermassive black hole.

Radio galaxies, quasars, supermassive black holes—in less than one hundred years, we've made many discoveries about black holes. The theory works and the evidence is good. The conclusions seem sound.

Still, all the evidence is indirect—like the sounds you hear when you shake a gift box. You might be sure you've figured out what's inside, but wouldn't you want to see if your guess was right?

Meet the Neighbors (and Then Some): Getting to Know a Few Black Holes

Thousands of objects either seem likely to be black holes or have reached "almost positive" confirmation as black holes. Some are close, some far. Some are small, others huge. Here are some black-hole highlights.

(False-color image)

Sagittarius A*

(Also known as Sgr A*. Read both as "Sagittarius A star.")

Type: Supermassive

Importance: The black hole at the center of our galaxy

Location: The center of the Milky Way galaxy, which is 27 thousand light years away, in the constellation Sagittarius

Cool fact: Today we know that Sagittarius A* is one of the mysterious radio sources that Grote Reber discovered with his homemade telescope. It's about 4 million times the mass of the Sun, and about as wide as Earth's orbit.

(False-color image)

NGC 5128

(Also known as Centaurus A)

Type: Supermassive

Importance: The black hole in the center of our nearest radio galaxy

Location: About 12 million light years away, in the constellation Centaurus

Cool fact: Two large lobes of radio energy appear on opposite sides of this giant black hole. Together, they span more than 800,000 light years, or about eight times the distance across our Milky Way galaxy.

V616 Monocerotis

(Also known as V616 Mon or A0620-00)

Type: Stellar mass

Importance: One of the closest known black holes to Earth

Location: About 3,460 light years away, in the constellation Monoceros, the Unicorn

Cool fact: This black hole was discovered in a flash—literally. On August 3, 1975, a satellite caught evidence of this black hole's presence as a burst of bright X-rays.

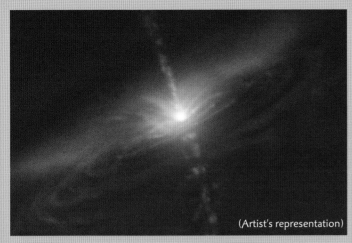

(Artist's representation)

Cygnus X-1

Type: Stellar mass

Importance: One of the smallest known black holes. Also, one of the first-ever black-hole candidates.

Location: About 6,000–8,000 light years away, in the "heart" of the constellation Cygnus

Cool fact: This black hole is so small that it would take less than an hour to drive the distance across it.

(False-color image)

M87*

(Also known as NGC 4486, Virgo A, or Pōwehi)

Type: Supermassive

Importance: Big and not too distant, M87* "appears" as the second-largest black hole in our sky, making it relatively easy to study.

Location: 55 million light years away, in the constellation Virgo.

Cool fact: The power of this supermassive giant extends well beyond its event horizon. High-energy material from just outside the black hole shoots away at tremendous speeds, resulting in shock waves tens of thousands of light years away. Also, M87* might go down in history as the most famous black hole ever. (Why? Turn the page.)

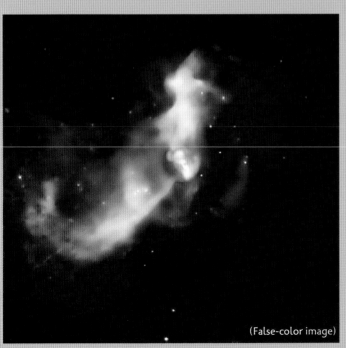

(False-color image)

Picturing a Black Hole

Scientists wanted to not see a black hole for themselves.

A picture of a black hole would be a game changer. It would offer direct evidence for black holes, the way unwrapping a present confirms or corrects your guess about what's inside. A picture might also lead to important discoveries about gravity, light, and matter, given that black holes are uniquely extreme.

Too bad black holes are invisible! It should be impossible to see one, let alone take its picture. Still, scientists wanted to give it a try.

Mission Impossible?

Not seeing is believing!

Radio telescopes like the Atacama Pathfinder Experiment (APEX), shown here, capture data from faraway objects in space. Could astronomers use such data to create a picture of a distant, invisible black hole?

Fueled by passion and a can-do (or at least a *maybe*-do) spirit, scientists launched the international Event Horizon Telescope project in 2009. EHT's ambitious mission: to take the first-ever picture of a black hole.

Well, kind of.

Technically, the EHT project was going for a picture of a black hole's surroundings, along with its central blackness, like a photo of an invisible person wearing a hoodie. The "hoodie" would be the glow of different types of light energy, such as X-rays and radio waves, released as matter spirals around the black hole. Could making some sort of ring-around-the-darkness portrait work?

Maybe, but it would be a long shot. A very long shot. After all, the closest black holes (that we know of) are thousands of light years away!

Going the Distance

Because of the distance, even a relatively nearby, gigantic black hole would appear minuscule from Earth. Getting a good, clear shot would require telescopic superpowers, like what you'd need to read a Parisian café menu from a New York deli. That's practically impossible—even if you know French.

Ouais! C'est impossible!

But scientists thrive in the realm of the "practically impossible," forging ahead in that little space between doable and not (yet). They've landed astronauts on the Moon, pinpointed planets around remote stars, even mapped the entire universe. Why not build a telescope big enough to image a black hole?

Because "big enough" would be too big—about as big across as Earth!

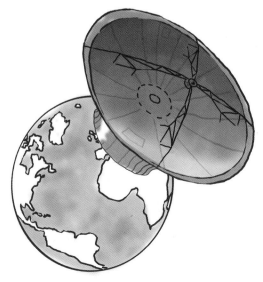

Dishing Up the Details

Undeterred, the EHT team had an idea. Radio telescopes were already stationed around the world. What if the team could link several of them together, precisely synchronizing them so they would work as one colossal instrument?

Imagine a giant telescope dish—one as wide as the Earth—with a small piece broken off. Even without that missing piece, a good image is possible. True, you'd have to fill in the gap with a reasonable guess—like envisioning a jigsaw puzzle's picture without all of its pieces in place. But you might still figure it out. Similarly, the EHT team hoped they could gather data from a network of telescopes and fill in any gaps to create a whole image.

Minding the Gaps

For this idea to work, EHT needed something else: cutting-edge computer software to help fill in the missing pieces. EHT assigned a specialized imaging team to tackle the challenge. This group would design the heart of the software—sets of rules, called algorithms, to control how computers would process the telescope data and complete the image.

But how would the team know if the resulting picture was accurate? After all, they were attempting to image something that had never been seen before.

To minimize the chances of error, the team tested the algorithms, using them to construct images of well-known objects and then making tweaks to improve the results. The team also planned to break into four smaller subgroups. Each subgroup would use its own algorithm and approach. What's more, it would work in secret—with no phone calls, texts, or knowing winks that might influence the others.

Afterward, they would reconvene and compare the four images to double-check their work. If the images checked out against each other, the team could confidently create one final picture.

Good to Go

Spring 2017. Eight years after the launch of the EHT project, a team of more than two hundred researchers was ready.

They had their super radio telescope: eight sites around the world, each equipped with a clock so accurate that in ten million years it would be off by only a second.

They knew where to aim the telescopes.

They had their software.

And they had a tight observing schedule. They couldn't hog so many telescopes indefinitely, so they were limited to ten nights to try for a picture.

Now the team needed one more thing: some good luck. They hoped their fine-tuned, complex system would operate glitch-free. They crossed their fingers for clear weather at *every* station, on each night. Could it, would it, all go right?

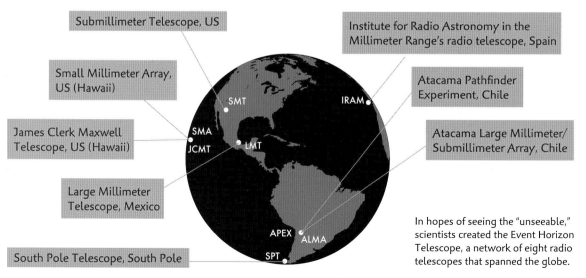

Submillimeter Telescope, US

Institute for Radio Astronomy in the Millimeter Range's radio telescope, Spain

Small Millimeter Array, US (Hawaii)

Atacama Pathfinder Experiment, Chile

James Clerk Maxwell Telescope, US (Hawaii)

Atacama Large Millimeter/ Submillimeter Array, Chile

Large Millimeter Telescope, Mexico

SMT
IRAM
SMA
JCMT
LMT
APEX
ALMA
SPT

In hopes of seeing the "unseeable," scientists created the Event Horizon Telescope, a network of eight radio telescopes that spanned the globe.

South Pole Telescope, South Pole

As Luck Would Have It

The team had just ten nights. In the end, they needed only four: four fabulous, flawless nights. On April 5, 6, 10, and 11, under clear skies, the telescopes faced the constellation Virgo and zeroed in on M87*, a black hole six and a half billion times the mass of the Sun.

Fifty-five million years ago, radio waves streamed from just outside M87*'s event horizon. Now, after crossing hundreds of trillions of miles, some of this very light silently landed on the telescope dishes, each bit of energy triggering an electrical impulse and registering as a morsel of data.

The telescopes gathered the ancient light. Then the observations were over. Everyone could pack up and go home.

And wait.

Over to You, Imaging Crew

Now it was up to the imaging team to work with the data—five petabytes, or five million gigabytes, in all. That's the equivalent of five thousand years of continuously streaming audio. Sending that much data over the internet would have taken too long. Instead, researchers stored it all in half a ton of computer components, which they sent across the globe by plane and truck to two central labs. The labs synced up the data from the different sites and—finally!—forwarded it to the imaging team. At last, the four independent subgroups could attempt an image of a black hole.

It took two years to ship and process the results. Finally, on April 10, 2019—a decade after the EHT project began—director Shep Doeleman announced, "We have seen what we thought was unseeable."

Then he revealed a picture.

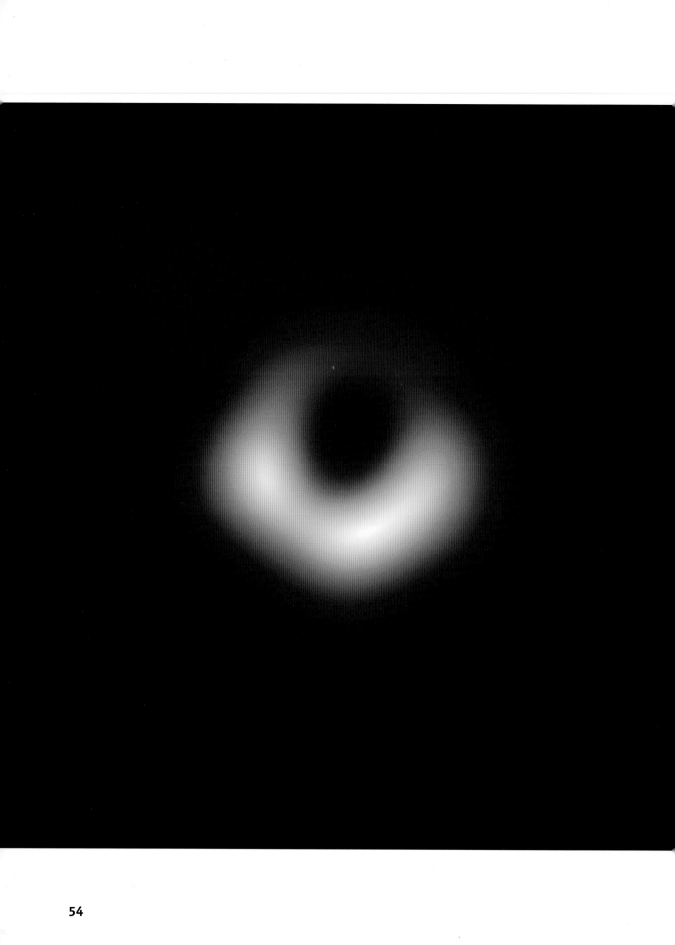

It's not an artist's illustration, not a computer-generated simulation. It's the real deal: an image created from data. In the picture, light from glowing matter surrounds absolute darkness, showing us a black hole's nothingness for the first time.

Applause. Tears. Dropped jaws and an around-the-world media blitz.

So much for mission impossible. Once again, scientists had pushed past no-can-do to achieve the seemingly unachievable.

And Yet . . .

For all the wonder of that accomplishment, for all the beauty of that picture, what's inside a black hole remains a mystery. We still don't know what's hidden just beyond that hoodie of light.

To find out, we'd have to visit a black hole, which seems *truly* impossible. Or is it? There is one way you could make the trip right now.

Tomorrow's News

It seems that every time you turn around, astronomers are announcing a new discovery about black holes. But this wasn't always the case. It took several decades to go from thinking black holes might exist to actually tracking one down. Only then did the pace of discovery pick up and the news start rolling in.

Scientists found supermassive black holes with the mass of millions or billions of Suns and figured out that such giants are at the center of most galaxies. They tracked matter falling into distant black holes and began unraveling how a black hole propels its high-energy jets. And they managed the incredible feat of taking the first black-hole picture.

You can be sure this isn't the be-all and end-all of black-hole science. In fact, this achievement marks the beginning of a new age of discovery. You are living in one of the most exciting times in black-hole astronomy. Just imagine what scientists might find out by the time you're twenty!

Stay tuned . . .

How about some "milk" with your tea? The hazy light of the Milky Way streams past the Teapot, a pattern of stars within the constellation Sagittarius. As viewed from Earth, the Teapot's spout points toward Sagittarius A*, the supermassive black hole at the very center of our galaxy.

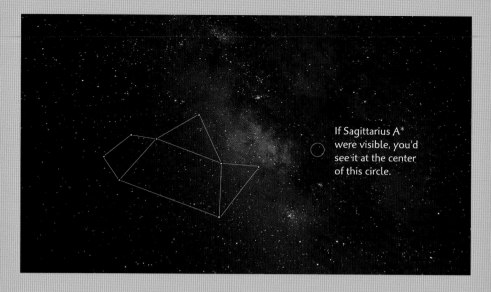

If Sagittarius A* were visible, you'd see it at the center of this circle.

The One That Got Away

M87* will go down in history as the first successfully imaged black hole. But there was another target on the 2017 imaging schedule: Sagittarius A* (Sgr A*)—the supermassive black hole at the center of our galaxy. What happened with Sgr A*?

The image was too fuzzy. Fast-moving patches of material orbit Sgr A* every few minutes. Their motion blurred the image, like when someone moves just as a picture is snapped. Also, any light heading our way has to travel through the relatively crowded galactic center. There, particles between the stars get in the way of the light. Like fog droplets, they make for a hazy image.

It takes a (worldwide) village. More than two hundred EHT team members from eighteen countries on six continents collaborated to turn the dream of a black-hole image into reality. About half of them posed for this photo, taken during a group meeting in the Netherlands.

A Picture of Teamwork

Just hours after the release of the picture of the black hole, EHT team member Katie Bouman found herself in the media spotlight. Headlines touted her as "the" person behind the picture. Many articles gave the impression that she single-handedly developed the computer code that helped produce the image of M87*. The young and brainy Bouman was definitely key to the project's success, but she wants the world to know that the real story is all about teamwork.

"No one . . . person made this image," she writes. "It required the amazing talent of a team of scientists from around the globe." In fact, about forty people were involved in the imaging effort, which was led by Bouman and her colleagues Andrew Chael, Kazunori Akiyama, Michael D. Johnson, Jose L. Gómez, and Sara Issaoun. Together the imaging team refined their strategies, developed the imaging algorithms, and made crucial decisions that helped turn data into the historic picture.

In April 2017, knowing that their work might lead to a historic black-hole image, this crew made time for a self-portrait. Standing in front of the Large Millimeter Telescope Alfonso Serrano (LMT) in Mexico, the team members are (from left to right) Aleksandar PopStefanija, Michael Janssen, Sandra Bustamante, Lindy Blackburn, Katie Bouman, Gopal Narayanan, and Edgar Castillo.

They embraced team spirit even when it came time to see the results. As Bouman recalls, at that magic moment, "a number of us . . . all squeezed into the room and pressed go on our computers at the exact same time. We didn't want any one person or algorithm to be the first one to make the image."

Close Encounters of the Imaginary Kind

A black hole is a destination—

for your imagination.

Unfortunately for the curious traveler, actually visiting a black hole in the near future is downright impossible. Even the nearest black holes are too far away.

For example, one of Earth's closest black-hole "neighbors" is about 3,460 light years away. (That's about 20 quadrillion miles, or 33 quadrillion kilometers.) No spacecraft is going to get you to a black hole and back by dinnertime—even if you live to be one hundred and only want dinner on your last day.

Luckily, you can visit a black hole with your imagination. Fueled by facts, you can blast off to a black hole or two and find out what might happen once you arrive.

The Closest‡ Black Hole to Earth?

If you were to aim a powerful-enough flashlight at the Moon, the light would arrive in a little more than a second. How long would it take to reach the nearest known black hole? The light from your super-flashlight would arrive at V616 Monocerotis (also called V616 Mon or A0620-00) in about 109 *billion* seconds, or 3,460 years.

‡Black-hole science is booming. By the time you read this, a different black hole may be deemed the closest. In 2020 the European Southern Observatory announced the discovery of a possible black hole only 1,000 light years away, in the star system HR 6819. If this object is confirmed as a black hole, it will be the new "closest"—until an even closer one is found.

What might happen to a spaceship approaching a black hole? (Artist's representation)

Are we there yet?

A Hole Variety of Places to Visit

As you take off, remember: predicting the exact details of your journey is tricky. After all, no one has ever visited a black hole, and we can't send a probe in to take a peek and send the information back to us. Not even sneak previews can escape from a black hole.

However, scientists have some best guesses about what could happen, based on what they know about gravity and black holes. A helpful rule of thumb is that close to the center of any black hole, every inch matters. Just a short distance can make an enormous difference in the strength of the black hole's gravitational effects.

The particulars of your adventure also depend on the type of black hole you visit. What size is it? Is it lumpy or smooth? Maybe it's a spinner?

Wish you were here!

Greetings From Cygnus X-1!

A spectacular view . . .

. . . of NGC 4486

Spinners, Lumpies, and Smoothies

When it comes to black holes, matter really matters. After all, if it weren't for all the matter crunched into a tiny space, an extreme gravity zone could never form. But it's not just *how much* matter in how small a space that makes a difference. *How* a star's matter collapses also affects the black hole that forms.

If the star was spinning before the collapse, then the black hole will spin, too. If the collapse is perfectly symmetric, a smooth black hole forms. On the other hand, even a slightly lopsided collapse leads to a lumpy black hole, with erratic gravitational effects. The gravity might be strong in some places and weak in others, and pull in different directions. However, a lumpy hole won't stay lumpy for long because its own gravity will work to smooth it out.

Beyond Your Brainy Blastoff:
Journey to a Black Hole

Suppose you were to visit a perfectly symmetric, smallish, non-spinning black hole. What would happen? Right away, you would need a new nickname—something like Stretch or the Spaghetti Kid. The pull from the black hole would force your body into a long, skinny, stringy shape. If you were going in feet first, your feet would stretch out the most. For a moment, they might look like droopy wet socks.

Not that you would notice any of this. By the time your toes could register "ouch" in your brain, your brain would not be working. This is the one time when stretching your mind might be a bad idea.

What if the black hole were lumpy? Instead of getting a nice, smooth stretch, you'd be pushed and pulled in changing directions, like human dough in a wrestling match with a pretzel maker. (The pretzel maker wins.)

Now **THAT'S** a stretch!

A kid visiting a black hole might be stretched out like spaghetti. Scientists call this phenomenon spaghettification, or the noodle effect. (Artist's representation)

Approaching the event horizon

After crossing the event horizon

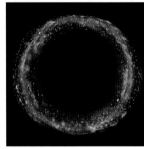

(Top: True-color image with false-color additions; middle and bottom: artist's representations)

So much for experiencing a smallish black hole; you'd have no time for sightseeing. A visit to a bigger black hole could be more interesting. It might take a while for the major effects to kick in. As you drifted in from the event horizon toward the singularity at the center, you might get a chance to look around.

What might you see? Even before you crossed the event horizon, things would start to look strange. The black hole would bend the light from all around and focus it in a miniature picture. Instead of seeing a sky full of stars, you'd see a tiny image of the black hole's surroundings, focused smack dab in the middle of the blackness overhead. Even stars on the opposite side of the black hole would be visible above you.

After you crossed the event horizon, the warped-sky image would distort even more. Now the light from everything outside the black hole would form a ring above you, like a halo overhead. Your sky would appear dark except for that bright circle—a ribbon of light that would get skinnier and skinnier as you continued to zoom inward.

You might want to tell the folks back home about all this. Ah well, too bad. Once across the event horizon, you wouldn't be able to get out any texts, calls, emails, smoke signals, or messages in bottles to spread the news.

It would be as if you were stuck in a one-way, sight-proof, soundproof bubble, sealed away from the rest of the universe. But there's no sense letting this tear you up. In a few hours, gravity will do the job instead.

Hmmm. Maybe you'd better turn that imagination of yours around and head back to Earth. That's the thing about thought experiments: they let you experience the impossible—and still get home in time for dinner.

Can you hear me now?

Well, usually. One of the best-ever thought experimenters missed more than a meal or two while on his mental adventures. "I am often so engrossed in my work that I forget to eat lunch," he wrote in a letter to his eleven-year-old son, just days before he unveiled one of his biggest ideas to a group of scientists. And what an engrossing, even bizarre idea it was! It took scientists on an incredible journey—a fantastic voyage through space and time that eventually led to black holes.

Ultimate FX?[‡]

Careening toward a singularity, you might have a colorful experience, if only for a blink of an eye. Picture the colors in a rainbow. Add the invisible light on either side—such as low-level infrared energy beyond red and high-energy X-rays beyond blue. Got it?

Now forget it. Viewed from in and near a black hole, colors can undergo some shifty effects, sliding from the red side of the rainbow toward the blue.

Yellow, green, and blue stars disappear—until you spot them with your X-ray detector. Meanwhile, new "stars" wink into view—balls of gas that glow in shifted infrared. Why? Light is distorted as it passes between places with different gravitation. The greater the difference, the greater the distortion. A black hole's extreme gravity intensifies this effect to the max.

Invisible radio, microwave, and infrared

Invisible ultraviolet, X-ray, and gamma

What you normally see: yellow

What you see from a black hole: nothing

The color of the star shifts as you approach the extreme gravity zone of the black hole. (Diagram not to scale)

Now try this tasty thought experiment. Say some friends far outside the black hole decide to send you a snack. If they launch a red apple your way, it's invisible to you at first. But keep your eyes peeled! Eventually, the apple shifts from invisible to blue, then to green, yellow, orange, and finally red, as it passes through gravitational zones that are closer and closer to the same strength as yours. Quick! Grab that apple before it disappears! Remember, once it whizzes past you, all its light continues in one direction, toward the center of the black hole, and you won't see it anymore.

[‡] Predictions like these are iffy. They are based on what scientists know about light and gravity. And they might be right—if the known laws of physics don't break down past the event horizon.

Turning the Universe Upside Down

A black hole is part of a strange new universe.

The scientist who forgot to eat his lunch was busy cooking up a whole new way of thinking about gravity. He was a radical smarty-pants—somebody with a wild imagination. Someone whose brain could surprise even himself.

Albert Einstein didn't *mean* to turn the universe upside down on everyone. He didn't *plan* on leading others to discover black holes. At first, all he set out to do was think about motion, along with a few other related ideas. But almost before he knew it, he had suddenly made our dependable old universe seem strange and new.

Just imagine being on an alien world and catching this view of a black hole in the night sky! Imagination has always helped open the door to new ideas in science. In fact, imagination led scientists to the idea of black holes. (Artist's representation)

Einstein's Spacey Ideas

Before Einstein, everyone pretty much thought of space as a sort of blank nothingness that separated objects like planets, solar systems, stars, and galaxies. This nothingness of space was a humongous, rigid background, with all of the matter in the universe arranged on it like pieces on a game board. Newton's force of gravity ruled this game, pulling things closer together and making them move against the spacey backdrop of nothingness.

But Einstein had his own ideas.

What if this background wasn't rigid? What if it wasn't nothingness?

What if it didn't stay the same all the time? What if, instead, space itself was something that changes—and even reacts to masses and matter?

Thanks to Einstein, we can imagine space as a blanket that stretches in response to every object's mass. A more massive object, such as the Earth, makes a deeper depression than a less massive object, such as the Moon. (Diagram not to scale)

In this way of thinking, the "background" acted more like a flexible mat, or a stretchy knit blanket. This new, blanket-like idea of space meant space could stretch, crunch up, bend, and warp. Moving objects would follow the curves of the blanket, moving along the surface through flat sections as well as distorted ones. This new idea about space changed the way scientists think about gravity.

Speaking of Gravity:
Newtonese and Einsteinese

Most of the time, gravity *seems* to work the way Newton described it. Newton's rules explain a lot, from falling apples to most planets' orbits. But his laws don't work perfectly. In high-gravity zones, Newton's ideas don't jibe with what scientists observe. For example, Mercury's orbit—up close to the Sun—has a blip in it that Newton's laws can't explain.

Glitches like this one were the reason Einstein worked so hard at coming up with a new explanation. He wanted to account for everything. His ideas about curving space may sound bizarre, but they work! They took care of the gaps in Newton's theory and explained Mercury's orbit. They led scientists to predict shifting starlight and black holes. All of this is powerful evidence that Einstein was onto something.

However, in day-to-day experience, the strangeness of Einstein's ideas doesn't help us, and Newton's notions do just fine. In everyday life, when gravity isn't especially intense, Newton's and Einstein's ways of thinking lead to similar results. The two explanations work like different languages that express the same thing. Is an apple red (English) or rojo (Spanish)? It's okay to use either description.

So we still use Newton's laws—even scientists do, much of the time. Sure, it's more exact to be Einsteinian and think of gravity as matter's effect on space. But it's all right to take a Newtonian shortcut and imagine gravity as a pull.

Gravity:

A Real Mind—and Space—Bender

In Einstein's way of thinking, what we see as gravitational "attraction" between two objects isn't really the effect of those objects pulling on each other. Instead, gravity is the effect that matter has on space itself.

Any material in space causes a distortion of some sort. A small concentration of matter results in a tiny dimple. A higher concentration makes a deeper dent. Each indentation is the gravity zone around the object.

Near the object, the distortion is greatest. The stretchy threads of the space fabric are bent by the effect of the mass on space. Farther and farther away, this effect is smaller and smaller, and so the threads are straighter and straighter.

A peanut would form a shallow dimple. If you could squash two peanuts together so they took up the same space as one, the dent would be slightly deeper. The deeper the dent, the steeper the gravity zone. It would take more energy for things to get out of the deeper dent.

From Einstein's Gravity to Black Holes

Einstein's idea of gravity had big consequences. It helped explain some observations that Newton's idea didn't account for. It also opened our minds to amazing new possibilities. For example, taking his cue from Einstein's idea that space bends, scientist Karl Schwarzschild began to think about what would happen if a place in space were extremely distorted. His answer: light would follow the hyper-bent space, never to turn away from it. This was the first prediction of a black hole. At first, some scientists (including Einstein!) rejected Schwarzschild's ideas. Others were intrigued and began searching the skies for real black holes. Just decades later, they found the first of them. It just goes to show: sometimes, as Einstein himself once said, "Imagination is more important than knowledge."

An elephant-packed peanut would be small and magnificently massive. It would cause a deep dent in the fabric of space. (Diagram not to scale)

The dense singularity at a black hole's center would be an extremely tiny but extremely heavy object placed on the blanket. Picture the supernova leftovers—the material that originally forms a black hole—as a peanut with all of the elephants in the world stuffed into it. Imagine placing that tremendously dense, elephant-stuffed peanut on a huge blanket. The blanket stretches and stretches, pulling out of shape. It forms not a shallow dimple in the blanket, but a steep well. A steep well that's really a lot like . . .

. . . a hole!

Glowing gas and dust whirl around a black hole. As they follow the dramatic curve in the fabric of space, they spiral along the steep gravity well that leads to the dense singularity at the center of the black hole. (Artist's representation)

So . . .
Even though a black hole is
NOT a hole—
at least not the kind you
can poke your finger through
or dig in the ground—
a black hole is NOT
exactly NOT a hole, either.

Is it?

Time Line

Discovering Black Holes

Discovering black holes took lots of brainpower, time, and technology. Here are some major milestones. One thing about this history of who-did-what-when: the list of scientists is not very diverse. Why? One big reason is that many people, including men of color and women, were generally excluded because of unfair ideas about race and gender. Today projects like the international EHT show that science is for everyone.

Sometime in the distant past

For the very first time, somebody doesn't just *notice* falling, but wonders about it. People from different cultures try to explain it—and keep trying until . . .

1687

English scientist and mathematician Isaac Newton writes about his ideas on gravity. He says it's a force that pulls objects together. (See pages 13–15.)

1783

1798

Separately, British scientist John Michell (in 1783) and French scientist Pierre-Simon Laplace (in 1798) speculate about Newton's idea of gravity and come up with an idea that people will later call "dark stars"—stars so massive that their light cannot shine out. (This notion is close to the idea of a black hole, but different.)

Late 1800s

By now scientists realize that Newton's rules for gravity don't explain everything. (For example, the planet Mercury doesn't move the way Newton's theory predicts.)

1905

German-born Swiss (and later American) scientist Albert Einstein publishes his ideas on time, space, and motion, which will lead to thinking about gravity in new ways.

(Artist's representation)

1915

Albert Einstein skips meals while putting the finishing touches on his full theory of gravity and motion, called the general theory of relativity. It includes a big idea: gravity is not a force! Instead, it is the bending effect that matter has on space. (See pages 66–69.)

1916

Karl Schwarzschild, a German scientist, is the first to see that if Einstein is right, black holes may exist—but he doesn't call them black holes. (See page 68.)

1919

Arthur Eddington, from England, and his international team of scientists observe that gravity can change the path of light, as predicted by Einstein's theory of general relativity. This is strong evidence that Einstein is onto something. (So Schwarzschild might be, too.) (See page 31.)

1933

American engineer Karl Jansky announces that radio waves are coming from outer space— and messing up phone lines, making them hiss. (See page 39.)

1939

Einstein writes about why he thinks Schwarzschild's proposed objects "do not exist." He rejects the idea of black holes!

Meanwhile, American scientists J. Robert Oppenheimer and Hartland Snyder figure out that some collapsing stars could lead to what we now call black holes.

1944

After years of studying the skies with his homemade radio telescope, American engineer Grote Reber begins publishing maps of the mysterious radio energy from outer space. The energy sources will later be known as radio galaxies. (See pages 39–40.)

1953

Using more powerful telescopes, Roger Jennison, from the UK, and Mrinal Das Gupta, from India, observe that Reber's energy sources are paired patches of radio energy around radio centers. (See page 40.)

1960

American scientists Allan Sandage and Thomas A. Matthews discover and photograph the first of a new type of strange radio object—later named a quasar. (See page 40.)

1963

Dutch-born Maarten Schmidt and American Jesse Greenstein realize that radio galaxies and quasars are very far away and must be emitting tremendous amounts of energy.

1964

Somebody—nobody can remember who—uses the term "black holes" at a scientific meeting. It doesn't catch on.

Yakov Zel'dovich, from the Soviet Union, and Austrian Australian American Edwin Salpeter suggest that something with a tremendous amount of mass may be powering the energy from quasars and radio galaxies.

1965

Briton Roger Penrose proves that if general relativity is correct, black holes must exist. (This proof paves the way to his 2020 Nobel Prize in Physics.)

1967

American scientist John A. Wheeler starts using the snappy phrase "black holes" to mean "gravitationally completely collapsed stars"—and this time the name catches on.

1969

British scientist Donald Lynden-Bell proposes that supermassive black holes may be the power source behind quasars and radio galaxies.

1971

The first possible black holes are identified with the help of X-ray telescope Uhuru. Observations of radio and visible light provide supporting evidence. One of the candidates is Cygnus X-1, orbiting a visible star. (See page 47.)

British scientist Stephen Hawking proposes that tiny black holes may exist. (These are later called micro or mini black holes.) (See page 43.)

1999

After lots of study, astronomers begin to agree: evidence suggests that most galaxies have a supermassive black hole at their center.

2001

American scientist Joseph F. Dolan announces the first observations of matter spiraling into a black hole, discovered by comparing two years of Hubble Space Telescope data from Cygnus X-1.

2015

A new instrument called LIGO detects evidence of two black holes colliding.

The present

You shine a flashlight out toward the nearest known black hole—V616 Monocerotis, in the direction of the constellation Monoceros, the Unicorn. (See page 59.)

1994

Measurements confirm the possibility of supermassive black holes. The "proof"? Using the Hubble Space Telescope, scientists led by Americans Richard Harms and Holland Ford find a disk of gas whipping around the center of galaxy M87. The gas is moving so fast that only a supermassive black hole—or some other, unknown object—can be at the center. (See pages 41–42.)

2002–2003

Finally! Thanks to new evidence gathered by several teams, scientists are generally convinced that a supermassive black hole is at the heart of the Milky Way. (See page 44.) This work earns two team leaders, Ghez and German scientist Reinhard Genzel, a 2020 Nobel Prize in Physics.

2019

Team EHT releases the first-ever picture of a black hole! (See page 54.)

5481
(Give or take a few years)

If the flashlight beam is strong enough and nothing interrupts its path, the light from the present arrives at V616 Monocerotis and crosses the event horizon.

2000

A team led by American scientist Andrea Ghez announces an extraordinary finding: some amazing force is whipping stars faster and faster around the center of the Milky Way. The team concludes that a supermassive black hole could explain this phenomenon.

2000

For the first time, observations reveal a "lone" stellar-mass black hole—like what Schwarzschild predicted in 1916. Before this, stellar-mass black holes had been found only as part of binary star systems.

2000

X-ray evidence reveals the first intermediate-mass black hole. (It's in the galaxy called M82.)

Glossary

Algorithm: In computer programming, a set of rules for a computer to follow so it can convert input to useful output. In EHT, algorithms were used to process telescope data (the input) to create a black hole image (the output).

Atom: The smallest amount you can have of a basic material, such as the smallest possible amount of copper in a penny. Every atom has a central part, called the nucleus, and one or more outer particles, called electrons.

Binary star: Two stars that orbit around each other. From far away, without a telescope, the two stars can look like one.

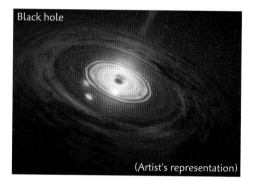

Black hole

(Artist's representation)

Black hole: A place in space with an extremely strong gravity zone that surrounds very dense matter in the center. The gravitational effect is so strong that once in this zone, nothing can exit—not even light.

Constellation: A pattern of stars that people have noticed and named. When we say that something is "in a constellation," that means it shows up in the same part of the sky as that star pattern.

Electron: One of the types of particles that make up an atom. Electrons are found outside the atom's nucleus.

Energy: The capacity to make things happen. For example, it takes energy to shake things up, heat them, and make them move. Energy comes in different forms, like sound, motion, visible light, X-rays, radio waves, and heat.

Event horizon: The boundary around a black hole that acts like a point of no return. Outside the boundary, it is possible for things to move away from the black hole. From inside the boundary, nothing can get back out.

Event Horizon Telescope (EHT): The network of radio telescopes used to create the first picture of a black hole.

Fallback: One way that a black hole can form. Fallback can happen after a supernova, when leftover star material falls back on itself, crunching into a tightly packed singularity.

False-color image: In astronomy, a color-coded map, often produced by a telescope. In telescope images, the colors represent light signals that are normally invisible to the human eye, such as radio waves and X-rays.

False-color image

Force: Any push or pull.

Friction: The motion of objects against each other, which results in their heating up. It can also mean a force that resists the motion of objects against each other.

Fusion: Melding, or blending two or more things to make one thing. Nuclear fusion happens when two atoms' centers (nuclei) are forced together and become one new nucleus. Fusing atoms can release a tremendous amount of energy. This energy is what keeps a star burning.

Galaxy: A group of billions and billions of stars, clustered together because of their gravitational effect on each other.

Galaxy

(True-color image with false-color additions)

Gravitas: The Latin name Isaac Newton used for gravity.

Gravitational lensing: A distorting effect that intense gravity can have on light. Gravitational lensing can make an image appear to be split, stretched, or multiplied.

Gravity: 1. According to Newton's theory, a naturally occurring pulling force between any two objects. 2. According to Einstein's theory, the bending effect that any matter has on the space around it, causing other matter to move toward it.

Intermediate black hole: A black hole with a mass in the range of hundreds to hundreds of thousands times the mass of the Sun.

Light: A form of energy. Light can be visible to human eyes, as in sunlight, or invisible, as in infrared light, radio waves, and X-rays.

Light year: The distance light can travel in one year, which is about 6 trillion miles (more than 9.5 trillion kilometers).

Mass: 1. The amount of material, matter, or substance that something contains. 2. Another word for matter.

Matter: Stuff, substance, or material.

Micro black hole or mini black hole: A microscopic black hole. Scientists think microscopic black holes may exist but have not found any (yet).

Neutron: One of the types of particles in the nucleus of an atom. Neutrons are also found in neutron stars.

Neutron star: An extremely dense star made of neutrons. A neutron star forms after the supernova phase of a very heavy star that is not quite massive enough to form a black hole. (The only thing known to be denser than a neutron star is a black hole.)

Neutron star

(Artist's representation)

Nuclear reaction: A high-energy interaction that takes place in or between atomic nuclei. One type of nuclear reaction, fusion, is what causes a star to shine.

Nuclei: The plural form of the word *nucleus*. Pronounced *NOO-klee-eye*.

Nucleus (of an atom): The tiny center part of an atom, containing small particles called protons and neutrons. A nucleus usually repels other nuclei.

Plasma: A very energetic form (or state) of matter. (Solid, liquid, and gas are other states of matter.) Plasma is found in stars, among other places. Like a liquid or gas, plasma has no definite shape and can move and flow freely. Plasma forms when a lot of energy is added to a gas, causing the electrons in its atoms to separate from their nuclei.

Quasar: A type of space object discovered in the 1960s with radio telescopes. The name "quasar" comes from the term "quasi-stellar radio source," meaning a radio source that seems *almost* like a star—but not quite. Scientists now think that each quasar is the energy streaming away from a supermassive black hole at the center of a galaxy, seen head-on. See *radio galaxy*.

Radio: A type of invisible light energy.

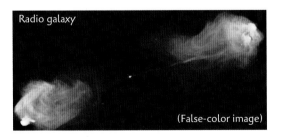

Radio galaxy

(False-color image)

Radio galaxy: A type of space object first mapped in the 1940s with radio signals. Radio galaxies are now known to be galaxies, each with a supermassive black hole at its center

and energy streaming off in opposite directions. Today radio galaxies' streamers of energy are thought to be the same thing as quasars, just seen from a different angle. (When we observe a radio galaxy, we are likely seeing a side-view of the streamers. A quasar is thought to be the head-on view.) See *quasar*.

Radio telescope: A telescope that works by detecting invisible radio waves instead of visible light. Based on the radio signals, radio telescopes create visible images, allowing people to see otherwise invisible information.

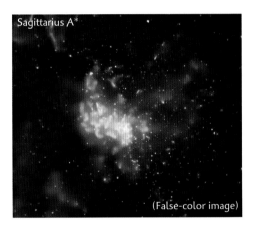

Sagittarius A*

(False-color image)

Sagittarius A*: The name given to the radio source at the center of the Milky Way galaxy, now known to be a black hole. Pronounced *saj-ih-TAIR-ee-us ay star*.

Singularity: The single point at the center of a black hole where all of its tremendously dense matter is concentrated. The rest of the black hole is the powerful gravity zone that surrounds this tiny spot.

Spaghettification: The distortion of any object into a long, skinny, spaghetti-like shape as it approaches a black hole. Sometimes called the noodle effect.

Star: A large, extremely hot ball of glowing gas and plasma.

Stellar: Having to do with stars.

Stellar-mass black hole: A black hole that forms when a massive star runs out of fuel. The original star is as massive as twenty-five to one hundred Suns, and the black hole it forms has three to ten times the mass of the Sun.

Supermassive black hole: A giant black hole—millions or billions of times the mass of the Sun—thought possibly to form from collisions of stars, galaxies, or smaller black holes, or a combination of these.

Supernova: 1. The end phase of some stars, which takes place after nuclear fusion stops. A supernova involves an inward collapse of star material, followed by a giant rebound, which makes the star extra bright and large. When conditions are right, a supernova becomes a black hole. 2. The event that takes place when a star becomes a supernova. You can talk about a star "going supernova" or say that a supernova is happening.

Supernova

(Artist's representation)

Thought experiment: A sort of mind game scientists play to help think through their ideas about how the universe works. Thought experiments can be especially useful when a real-life experiment would be difficult or impossible. The scientist imagines a set of circumstances and then tries to figure out what would happen next. For example, a scientist might think, "Suppose a person could visit a black hole and survive. What would that person see?"

Ultramassive black hole: The most massive type of black hole thought to exist, having ten billion or more times the mass of the Sun.

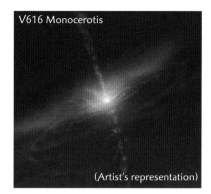

V616 Monocerotis

(Artist's representation)

V616 Monocerotis (also called V616 Mon or A0260-00): The closest known black hole to Earth, about 3,460 light years away in the direction of the constellation Monoceros, the Unicorn. "Monocerotis" is pronounced *muh-NAH-ser-OH-tis*.

White dwarf: The cooling end phase of a star that does not become a supernova. From Earth, white dwarfs seem dim, small, and whitish. Close up, though, they are intensely bright.

X-ray: A highly energetic form of light that is invisible to human eyes.

X-ray telescope: A telescope that works by detecting invisible X-rays instead of visible light. Based on the X-ray signals, X-ray telescopes create visible images, allowing people to see otherwise invisible information.

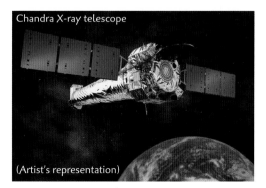

Chandra X-ray telescope

(Artist's representation)

Author's Note

How Do You Know I Know?

Whenever you read nonfiction, it's a good idea to check what the author has to say about how she or he found out about the topic. It helps you figure out how reliable the information is. (However, even reliable work gets outdated—especially in science, where new discoveries can dramatically change things.)

So, where did I find my facts and figures? In lots of different places. Tracking down black-hole information was a little like tracking black holes. It took research, questions, and lots of cross-checking to piece together something that made sense. Still, it was much easier for me to find information than for astronomers to locate black holes. Helpful librarians, such as Jeffrey Mehigan and Debbie Batson, ensured I found what I wanted—without special X-ray detectors.

You know you've relied on a book when you find cookie crumbs in the binding. While I was researching this book, my most-crumb-filled volume was *Black Holes & Time Warps: Einstein's Outrageous Legacy* by Kip Thorne. There must also be virtual cookie bits in my digital edition of Seth Fletcher's *Einstein's Shadow: A Black Hole, a Band of Astronomers, and the Quest to See the Unseeable*, which details decades of effort leading up to EHT's "impossible" black-hole image.

I learned some basics from general science magazines, such as *Scientific American, Astronomy*, and *Sky & Telescope*. Their articles led me to others, including numerous scientific papers.

It's terrific fun to read what the original thinkers had to say for themselves. I read parts of Albert Einstein's *Relativity: The Special and General Theory* and found his letter about forgetting to eat lunch in *Einstein: His Life and Universe* by Walter Isaacson. Isaac Newton's *Principia:*

The Mathematical Principles of Natural Philosophy (translated by Andrew Motte) allowed me to see what Newton himself thought. And, of course, witnessing EHT's historic announcement was a thrill. The team's talks and articles educated and inspired me. Katie Bouman's social media posts from April 10, 2019, quoted in chapter 7, made me feel almost like I'd been there, glimpsing the imaging team's first results. (I wish!)

Naturally, I am careful to choose reliable websites. For this book, I scouted out information on sites published by science news organizations, NASA, the European Space Agency, and observatories such as the Chandra X-ray Observatory.

It's important for me to talk with people who deeply understand the relevant science. Dr. Wendy Hagen Bauer, now Wellesley College professor emerita of astronomy, graciously served as expert reader and advisor. I remain grateful for her impressive dedication and attention to detail, and to the other scientists she consulted.

For this edition, EHT scientists Richard Anantua, Mislav Baloković, Katie Bouman, Alan Roy, and Fumie Tazaki generously offered support and feedback on chapter 7. Also, my husband, Barry, was especially helpful. He dug up articles, checked facts, and helped me resolve picky details and big ideas. University of Southern Maine astronomer and planetarium manager Edward Gleason kindly read a draft of chapter 7 and answered my questions—while running the planetarium during a pandemic and welcoming his infant daughter. (Amazing.) Software engineer Mike Bitner helped me tackle writing about algorithms. Thank you, all.

Of course, even with all these resources and helpful people, I may have made errors. If they exist, I hope they are few and far between, but if you find any, they are mine, all mine!

Resources

Books

Asimov, Isaac. *How Did We Find Out About Black Holes?* New York: Walker and Company, 1978.
This oldie is still a goody. Isaac Asimov writes in clear detail about key discoveries related to black holes.

Carson, Mary Kay. *Beyond the Solar System: Exploring Galaxies, Black Holes, Alien Planets, and More: A History with 21 Activities*. Chicago: Chicago Review Press, 2013.
If you find black holes totally absorbing, you may want to find out more about other space objects, too. Activities help you explore space without having to pack for the trip.

DeCristofano, Carolyn Cinami. *Ultimate Space Atlas*. Washington, DC: National Geographic, 2017.
Now that you know about black holes, explore the rest of the universe!

Jackson, Ellen. *The Mysterious Universe: Supernovae, Dark Energy, and Black Holes*. Boston: Houghton Mifflin Harcourt, 2011.
The universe has room for lots of cool phenomena.

MacLeod, Elizabeth. *Albert Einstein: A Life of Genius*. Toronto: Kids Can Press, 2003.
Find out about Einstein and his ideas in this biography.

Websites

The websites listed below were current at the time of publication. To find out more about black holes, try searching for "black hole" using your favorite search engine.

Chandra X-ray Observatory
http://chandra.harvard.edu
Marvel at images of supernovae and other intergalactic wonders exposed by the X-ray vision of the Chandra telescope.

ESA Kids
https://www.esa.int/kids/
This website from the European Space Agency lets you explore space from the comfort of a computer. Take off by searching for "black holes."

Event Horizon Telescope Videos
https://eventhorizontelescope.org/videos
Videos include a greeting from an EHT observing team and an imaginary trip with real pictures that zoom in on M87*.

NASA's Imagine the Universe!
http://imagine.gsfc.nasa.gov/docs/science/science.html
Dig deeper into the physics and astronomy of black holes (and more).

Science News for Students
https://www.sciencenewsforstudents.org
Stay up-to-date on black-hole science in the news. Start by searching for "black holes."

Image Credits

Chapter 1
p. 4: NASA/Chandra X-ray Center (CXC)/M. Weiss
pp. 6–7: NASA/Jet Propulsion Laboratory (JPL)
p. 10: NASA/Dana Berry, SkyWorks Digital

Chapter 2
p. 12: NASA/JPL

Chapter 3
p. 18: Chandra: NASA/Spitzer/Harvard-Smithsonian Center for Astrophysics (CfA)/L. Allen
p. 21: Solar and Heliospheric Observatory (SOHO) (European Space Agency [ESA] and NASA)
p. 22: NASA/Goddard Space Flight Center (GSFC)/Dana Berry
p. 23: Image and text © 1989–2010, Australian Astronomical Observatory (AAO), photograph by David Malin
p. 25 (top): European Southern Observatory (ESO)/A. Roquette

Chapter 4
p. 26: NASA and G. Bacon (Space Telescope Science Institute [STScI])

Chapter 5
p. 32: Hubble and Chandra image credit: NASA, ESA, CXC, STScI, and B. McNamara (University of Waterloo); Very Large Array Telescope image credit: National Radio Astronomy Observatory (NRAO), and L. Birzan and team (Ohio University)
p. 35: W. N. Colley and E. Turner (Princeton University), J. A. Tyson (Bell Labs, Lucent Technologies), and NASA
p. 36: ESA, NASA, and Felix Mirabel (French Atomic Energy Commission and Institute for Astronomy and Space Physics/Conicet of Argentina)

Chapter 6
p. 40: NRAO/Associated Universities, Inc. (AUI)/National Science Foundation (NSF)
p. 41 (bottom): NRAO/AUI/NSF
p. 42: NASA/JPL
p. 44 (bottom): X-ray: NASA/CXC/University of Massachusetts (UMass)/D. Wang, et al.; Optical: NASA/ESA/STScI/D. Wang, et al.; Infrared: NASA/JPL-Caltech/Spitzer Science Center (SSC)/S. Stolovy
p. 45: X-ray: NASA/CXC/Massachusetts Institute of Technology (MIT)/C. Canizares, M. Nowak; Optical: NASA/STScI

p. 46 (top): NASA/CXC/MIT/F. K. Baganoff, et al.
p. 46 (bottom): NASA/CXC/CfA/R. Kraft, et al.
p. 47 (middle): NASA/CXC/Smithsonian Astrophysical Observatory (SAO)
p. 47 (bottom): X-ray: NASA/CXC/Kavli Institute for Particle Astrophysics and Cosmology (KIPAC)/N. Werner, E. Million, et al.; Radio: NRAO/AUI/NSF/F. Owen

Chapter 7
p. 48: ESO/B. Tafreshi (https://twanight.org)
p. 54: Event Horizon Telescope (EHT) Collaboration
p. 56 (top): Image by User: Moondigger; overlay by Barry DeCristofano
p. 57 (top): Ana Torres Campos
pp. 56–57: Dick van Aalst, Radboud University

Chapter 8
p. 62 (top): R. Williams (STScI), the Hubble Deep Field Team, and NASA

Time Line
pp. 72–75: NASA and G. Bacon (STScI)

Glossary
p. 76 (left): NASA/Dana Berry, SkyWorks Digital
p. 76 (bottom right): Hubble and Chandra image credit: NASA, ESA, CXC, STScI, and B. McNamara (University of Waterloo); Very Large Array Telescope image credit: NRAO, and L. Birzan and team (Ohio University)
p. 77 (left): Hubble image: NASA, ESA, K. Kuntz (Johns Hopkins University), F. Bresolin (University of Hawaii), J. Trauger (JPL), J. Mould (National Optical Astronomy Observatory (NOAO), Y.-H. Chu (University of Illinois, Urbana), and STScI; CFHT image: Canada-France-Hawaii Telescope/J.-C. Cuillandre/Coelum; NOAO image: G. Jacoby, B. Bohannan, M. Hanna/NOAO/Association of Universities for Research in Astronomy (AURA)/NSF
p. 78 (left): NRAO/AUI/NSF
p. 78 (right): NASA/CXC/MIT/F. K. Baganoff, et al.
p. 79 (left): NASA/GSFC/Dana Berry
p. 79 (bottom right): NASA/CXC/Next Generation Space Telescope (NGST)

All other images created by Michael Carroll.

Index